W9-BCK-635

OMNIVM LVX CIVIVM

BOSTON
PUBLIC
LIBRARY

GOVERNMENT
and the
ENVIRONMENT
Tracking the Record

Thomas G. Aylesworth

ENSLOW PUBLISHERS, INC.

Bloy St. & Ramsey Ave.   P.O. Box 38
Box 777   Aldershot
Hillside, NJ 07205   Hants GU12 6BP
U.S.A.   U.K.

Copyright © 1993 by Enslow Publishers, Inc.

All rights reserved.

No part of this book may be reproduced by any means
without the written permission of the publisher.

Library of Congress Cataloging-in-Publication Data
    Aylesworth, Thomas G.
    Government and the environment: tracking the record/Thomas G.
Aylesworth.
        p. cm.—(Better earth)
    Includes bibliographical references and index.
    Summary: Describes the many aspects of environmental pollution,
the growing awareness of the problem, and the role of the federal
government in formulating a policy to protect the environment.
    ISBN 0-89490-400-0
    1. Environmental policy—United States—Juvenile literature.
2. Environmental policy—United States—States—Juvenile literature.
[1. Environmental policy. 2. Environmental protection.] I. Title.
II. Series: Better earth series.
HC110.E5A95   1993
363.7'056'0973—dc20   92-24515
                                       CIP
                                       AC

Printed in the United State of America

10 9 8 7 6 5 4 3 2 1

Illustration Credits:

AP/Wide World Photos, p. 43; Environmental Protection Agency, p. 4,
7, 12, 16, 20, 25, 27, 35, 36, 38, 47, 50, 54, 57, 71, 74, 82, 89.

Cover Photo: Environmental Protection Agency

CONTENTS

Trash may be ugly, especially when it builds up in our environment.

Preface

The need for a national concern about the environment probably began to be more widely realized in 1962. It was an innocent year in a more innocent time, and few people were very worried about protecting our planet. But it was also the year in which Rachel Carson's brilliant book *The Silent Spring* was published. She warned that careless use of weed killers and insecticides created a hazard to wildlife and to human beings. Even though most people turned a deaf ear, her book excited some and was the beginning of many studies of the environment. Here is where we were in 1962 and how far we have come.

Trash

Our roadsides were pretty messy, many of them cluttered with bottles, soda cans, and other items of trash dumped by motorists. Today most states have litter laws to fine offenders. There have even been a few judges, most notably in Michigan, who sentenced litterbugs to go out to the highway and personally clean up a stretch of the roadside.

Several states have passed so-called "bottle bills," which require deposits on all plastic and metal soda and beer containers. When the empties are brought back to a redemption center, the customer can get back his or her deposit—five cents in Connecticut, Delaware, Iowa, Maine, Massachusetts, New York, Oregon, and Vermont; ten cents in Michigan; or a redemption value in California. Our highways are much cleaner.

In the early 1960s, almost nobody recycled anything. All those clear, brown, and green glass bottles and jars, all those juice, soda, water, milk, and laundry detergent plastic bottles, all those aluminum and tin food and beverage cans and clean aluminum food trays, all those old newspapers were just lumped together and taken to a dump or a landfill.

Today, all across the country, you can buy products bearing the familiar recycling triangle. States and towns and cities have started recycling, and recycling cans and cases can be seen once a week at curbsides all over the United States.

Air

Automobiles everywhere were belching unclean air as they burned their (often leaded) gasoline. Today some states have set up an annual required emission test for most automobiles, and many motorists are forced to have their car engines repaired if they fail that examination.

In the 1960s, we were still spraying the pesticide DDT (dichloro-diphenyl-trichloroethane) to kill obnoxious insects and other small pests. This substance, which was found to cause cancers in laboratory animals, has been banned in the United States since 1972.

Home

In the autumn, the smell of burning leaves was ever-present as home owners set fire to their tree debris at the curbside. This polluted the air and added to the smog that was so

The triangle that tells you something can be recycled. On such items as plastic bottles, a number can be found in the center that indicates what kind of plastic it is and how it can be recycled.

common. Today most towns and cities have outlawed this practice, and the leaves are picked up (either by the home owner or the town) and hauled to a central disposal plant.

Homes and public buildings were regularly insulated with asbestos—in the walls and around the pipes. It wasn't until 1970 that asbestos was banned in the United States because of its cancer-causing threat.

Other Problems

In the 1960s, most Americans were unaware of some of the pollution problems that we hear about every day in the 1990s. Today there is radon testing of homes and the development of a genetically engineered, non-polluting pesticide. Campaigns to preserve the ozone layer, remove asbestos, and cut back on acid rain are recent, as is our concern with industrial pollution of bodies of water.

Government's Role

These concerns are so far-reaching that sometimes individual efforts alone are not enough to correct the problems. But they can be corrected by various governments. Some of the concerns, such as garbage and trash pollution, can be handled by town and city governments. Larger problems, such as lake water pollution, need the efforts of the states. Since air pollution and the pollution of interstate water for example, know no boundaries, they must be controlled by the federal government. Finally, such vast problems as acid rain and ocean pollution require the cooperation of the governments of many countries.

These days we have really become aware of how important it is to save our planet. It may appear that things are getting worse, but perhaps that is because we are more aware of pollution than we were. The main thing is that individuals and governments are working harder to make things better. Of course, sometimes the problems seem overwhelming. But we, and our governments, can win—if we work at it.

1
Our
Polluted World

People, animals, and plants have always polluted the environment with various kinds of waste. But in ancient times, it was not much of a problem. Even though human waste polluted the soil and the water, and smoke from fires polluted the air, people were not crowded together. Most of them lived in rural areas, so their waste products were scattered and did not build up in one place. And the human population was much smaller then. Also, it was a time without pollution-creating machinery.

Over a long period of time, large numbers of people began living together in growing cities. With the cities getting larger, pollutants increased and were created and piled up in a smaller area.

Industries Appear

Then came what is called the Industrial Revolution in the 1700s and early 1800s. People were living closer together to work in the factories that were being built. More human waste was accumulating, and since the factories relied on coal, the air was being polluted at a tremendous rate. Polluted water containing raw sewage caused such diseases as typhoid fever.

In the early 1900s, the automobile appeared, as did other polluting devices and processes. In the 1930s, smoke and soot caused by steel mills, power plants, railroads, and heating plants were spewing into the air over most cities in the East and the Midwest. Drivers in some cities, most notably Pittsburgh and St. Louis, often had to use their headlights in the middle of the day.

By the middle of this century, there were pollution problems in almost every lake, stream, and river and in the air over every city in the United States. But fortunately, in the 1950s, some people began to worry about their pollution problems and began to do something about them.

What Do Americans Think?

Are people really pollution-conscious today? First the good news. In a 1991 *New York Times*/CBS (Columbia Broadcasting System) poll, people were asked: For the country as a whole, is pollution a serious problem that's getting

Smog can be found hovering over many of our cities. The sign beside this highway indicates that special lanes have been set aside for cars with three or more passengers, in an effort to reduce the number of automobiles on the road.

worse, a problem but one that is not so serious, or not much of a problem? The results:

Serious—84 percent

Not so serious—11 percent

Not much of a problem—3 percent

Don't know—2 percent

It looked as though these people were really pollution-conscious.

Now the bad news. In the same poll, the same people were asked: How serious a problem do you think pollution is in the area where you live—a serious problem that's getting worse, a problem but one that is not so serious, or not much of a problem? The results:

Serious—42 percent

Not so serious—29 percent

Not much of a problem—27 percent

Don't know—1 percent[1]

It would seem that a lot of people don't recognize pollution when they see it in their own neighborhoods. And that is one of the most important reasons why government needs to be involved in pollution fighting. The average person may not be aware of pollution conditions, and it takes an experienced authority to monitor the environment. Besides, there are so many kinds of pollution that individuals cannot keep track of them all.

Air

Air pollution harms or even kills plants and animals, and it can also damage all sorts of property. All over the world, it is eating away at homes, other buildings, and outdoor statues. This type of pollution is caused by the particulates that are given off into the air. Particulates are tiny particles of solid or liquid matter.

About 85 percent of our air pollution is caused by the burning of fossil fuels such as coal and gas. Most of this comes from automobiles, but fossil-fuel power plants also contribute pollutants. The pollutants are carbon monoxide, sulfur oxides, nitrogen oxides, hydrocarbons, and particulate matter.

Winds can blow the particulates away, and rain can carry them back to the earth, but neither can get rid of them. When a layer of warm air settles over a ground-level layer of cold air, as happens in such cities as Los Angeles and Mexico City, a thermal inversion is caused. The warm air holds down the cool air, and the pollutants in the cool air cannot be scattered by the wind. The result is smog—a combination of smoke and fog.

In humans, this can cause burning of the eyes and lung irritation. If it settles in the lungs, it can make people suffering from asthma and bronchitis even sicker. Many scientists believe that smog particulates are direct causes of certain cancers, emphysema, and pneumonia.

As to plants, these particulates can stunt the growth of, or even kill, almost any of them. Particulates have wiped out whole orange groves, vegetable gardens, and forests.

Almost any material gets dirtier and wears out faster in the presence of polluted air. This air can even eat away stone, concrete, and steel.

The weather may be changed by polluted air, too. Particulates can scatter the rays of the sun, causing a lessening of the light that gets to the ground. This can cause the average temperatures to fall. The opposite result can be caused by carbon dioxide and other gases in what is called the greenhouse effect. This happens when the gases let the heat from the sun filter through to the ground but prevent the heat from rising and going back into space. This can cause the average temperature to rise.

Water

Water pollution cuts down on the amount of water that can be used by people for drinking, cleaning, and such things as swimming and fishing. Most of the pollutants in the water come from industrial plants, farms, and sewage systems.

Industrial pollution consists mainly of chemicals, wastes from animal and plant matter, and some other sources. Farm pollutants are mainly animal waste, fertilizers, and pesticides. Sewage pollution comes from the wastes from homes, offices, and industries. Both industrial and sewage pollution can include what is called thermal

Polluted water is not only foul-looking, it can also represent a health hazard to plants and animals.

pollution. This occurs when heated water is added to a natural body of water. This heated water can change the temperature of the body of water and kill animals and plants. Another serious water pollutant is oil, which ruins beaches and kills animals and plants.

Soil

Soil pollution ruins the thin layer of topsoil that has taken thousands of years to form. Excess fertilizer may kill the soil bacteria that are so important in making more topsoil. Pesticides can also kill other helpful organisms.

Another problem with soil is erosion. This is the wearing away of soil and can be caused by the removal of trees and other plants whose roots keep the soil in place. Then the wind can blow the soil away or rain can wash it away. Most erosion is the result of poor farming methods or the clearing of land for roads or the construction of real estate developments, such as shopping malls or houses.

Solid Waste

Solid waste pollution is most visible as litter beside the road, garbage in dumps, and junk floating in lakes, ponds, and streams. Solid wastes come in all shapes and sizes—junked automobiles, food cans, paper and packaging materials, and slag heaps with cinders of metallic waste. The big problem with solid wastes is not that they are ugly, although they certainly are, it is that they are hard to dispose of. Burning them can cause air pollution. Storing them in dumps provides a home for rats, cockroaches, and other pests.

There was a time when most food cans were made of tin or steel that would eventually rust away and be absorbed by the soil. But aluminum is replacing those materials, and aluminum stays in its original state for many years. Also, cardboard packaging that decays gradually has been replaced by plastics that will not decay and, when burned, give off harmful gases.

Other Pollution

Other kinds of pollution are varied indeed. Noise, for example, is a serious problem, especially in cities. Factories, portable radios, construction machinery, and airplanes, cars, trucks, motorcycles, trains, and buses are almost constantly assaulting our ears. Too much noise can cause hearing problems or even deafness, and it can also contribute to high blood pressure and ulcers because of the stress it causes.

Radiation is another invisible pollutant. Some of it comes from the sun and other outer space sources. Some of it comes from radioactive fallout from nuclear weapons testing and nuclear power plants. Some electronic devices, such as lasers, x-ray machines, color television sets, and microwave ovens, produce radioactivity. Exposure to large amounts of radiation can lead to cancer and serious changes in reproductive cells.

Acid rain has become more and more of a pollution problem. Acid rain is not new. It dates back more than 150 years—since coal was first burned on a large scale to produce power. It is caused by nitrogen oxide and sulfur dioxide from automobiles, factories, and power plants that burn oil or coal. These gases react with the moisture in the air, and the results are nitric and sulfuric acid.

These acids can be caught in high wind currents and blown through the atmosphere — sometimes hundreds of miles away. The pollutants drift with the clouds until rain washes them from the air.

When this rain falls into lakes, streams, and rivers, fish cannot produce any young. Birds that feed on the fish and insects are next to go.

Acid rain also pollutes soil, resulting in the killing of crops and the loss of fertility in the soil. Since weather needs no passport, the acid rain may travel long distances, even across international borders.

Pesticides are important to all people. But unfortunately, many of them may never reach the pest they are supposed to kill. Pesticide particles may travel through the air and on the land or water, where they remain, never contacting the pests. If a human or other animal comes in contact with the particles, the pesticides can be absorbed and end up in body tissues and organs. When people or other animals eat plants or animals that contain pesticides, the poisons are passed along. Scientists tell us that these

A small part of a fish kill. These dead fish were overcome by pollution in the water.

have caused the deaths of countless birds, fish, and other animals.

Some heavy metals, such as mercury or lead, pollute the water, air, and soil as solids, liquids, or gasses. Most of this type of pollution is caused by industrial or motor vehicle waste. Metallic pollution can spread over large areas and is capable of lasting for a long time. And, like pesticides, it can collect in the tissues and organs of animals. Many metals are poisonous and in large amounts can cause damage to the nervous system.

Obviously, with all these pollution problems, governments had to step in.

2
The Federal Government Begins the Fight

The first important environmental law passed by the Congress of the United States was enacted in 1899. It was called the Rivers and Harbors Act, and its purpose was to outlaw the dumping of liquid wastes (except for sewage) into navigable waters. It would have been a big help, but it was not, for the most part, enforced. Since that time, governments have done a better job.[1]

It was not until 1948, however, that a more comprehensive environmental law was passed. This was the Water Pollution Control Act. It gave power to the Department of the Interior to force water polluters to develop antipollution measures. Another function of this act was to give federal money to local governments to build sewage treatment plants.

The 1950s

The Air Pollution Control Act was passed by Congress in 1955. Power was given to the Public Health Service to start research in air pollution and give technical assistance to state and local governments.

More attention to water pollution came in 1956 when Congress passed the Federal Water Pollution Control Act. It added more help for local governments by giving them planning and technical assistance and research and construction grant money for waste-treatment plants.

The 1960s

So far, so good. But there were some embarrassing problems occurring, such as the time when the horribly polluted Cuyahoga River near Cleveland caught fire.

So the Water Pollution Control Act of 1956 was amended in 1961. The amendments gave the federal government the responsibility of enforcing the pollution laws in waters that were shared by two or more states (rivers such as the Hudson and some of the Great Lakes, for example) as well as coastal waters. Additional funds were set aside for federal construction grants.

The Clean Air Act was enacted by Congress in 1963. It made provisions for federal grants to local and private agencies searching for new ways of air pollution control. The act also gave the federal government the authority to begin work on interstate air pollution problems. This was the first law that let the federal government take some action to control air pollution from smokestacks, such as those of steel mills and metal producing factories. It was strengthened by amendments in 1965, when the Department of Health, Education and Welfare (HEW, now the Department of Health and Human Services) was given the task of setting emissions standards for new cars.

Also in 1965 came more amendments to the Water Pollution Control Act. Congress set up the Federal Water Pollution Control Administration, which took over the pollution control duties of the Public Health Administration (a part of HEW). The amendments, in addition, called for a timetable for the cleanup of interstate and coastal waters.

That was a banner year for Federal environmental laws. Another law passed in 1965 by Congress was the Solid Waste Disposal Act. It was designed to find better ways to dispose of solid waste and various state and local programs for the disposal of these wastes. The control of the funds was given jointly to HEW and the Department of the Interior.

The Clean Air Act of 1967 extended federal government's role in setting and overseeing the standards for auto emissions. The 1967 Air Quality Act gave HEW the power to enforce air quality standards in areas that were severely polluted. States thus had to begin air cleanup plans or be prosecuted by the government.

Smoke belching from factory chimneys — one of the chief causes of air pollution in our industrial society.

In 1966 the federal standards for hydrocarbons (chemical compounds consisting only of hydrogen and carbon) and carbon monoxide (a colorless, odorless, poisonous gas) in automobile exhausts were established, and they were to go into effect with the 1968 model year. This made automakers start developing engines that would use unleaded gasoline.

In 1969 HEW formulated guidelines for the maximum levels of sulfur dioxide and suspended particulates coming from industrial installations. And on February 2, 1969, came the first lawsuit under the Clean Air Act. This suit was filed in Baltimore, Maryland, to close a plant that melted animal fats for industrial use. The plant had violated pollution standards.

Congress passed the Environmental Policy Act in 1969. This required every United States government agency planning a project to file an assessment of its impact on the environment. Most state and local planning agencies now also require an environmental impact statement.

An environmental impact statement is a report prepared for all projects and programs that might affect the environment. The statement is issued by any agency of the federal government that plans to build such facilities as dams, highways, and power plants. The federal agency must also issue a report for any large state, local, or private project that it will support financially or regulate.

In 1969 President Richard M. Nixon established the Environmental Quality Council (EQC) by executive

Diesel fumes emerging from the exhaust of a city bus. The emissions from motor vehicles add to the air pollution problems in the civilized world.

order. It was to be a cabinet-level group set up to give advice on the efforts to preserve, as Nixon said, "the availability of good air and good water, of open space and even quiet neighborhoods." Nixon was to head the group himself.

The executive order also suggested a fifteen-member Citizens Advisory Committee on Environmental Quality. But Congress resisted the idea, calling the EQC an inefficient way of solving problems. So Congress enacted the National Environmental Policy Act (NEPA), attempting to formulate a national policy on environmental protection.

In the autumn of 1969, the government began to crack down on water polluters, such as a mining company, several steel mills, and even the city of Toledo, Ohio, which was caught polluting Lake Erie. The state of Iowa was also ordered to treat all its sewage that had been flowing into the Missouri and Mississippi rivers. This was the first time that the federal government had used the power of the Water Quality Act to tell a whole state what to do.

Continuing Problems

Various governments have to get involved in pollution control because there are too many causes of the problem for individuals or small groups to handle. Basically, there are three human causes of pollution—technological, economic, and social.

Many technological advances in transportation, industry, and agriculture have made life better, but they have caused a great deal of pollution. As automobiles became more powerful, they produced more and more harmful gases.

Sewage treatment plants, although they are designed to protect the environment, can also pollute it. Most treatment plants remove dangerous animal and plant waste by using bacteria and oxygen to break down chemically the wastes and make them into organic nutrients. But these nutrients are sometimes put in the water, and they increase the growth of tiny water plants, which may compete with other plants and animals.

The increased use of plastics is also a problem. Not only do they not degrade, but also the manufacture of plastic requires a great deal of electric power, thus putting a strain on power plants. Then the power plants that burn coal or oil contribute more air-polluting particles.

The economic causes of pollution are based on the lack of desire by most people to spend money. It can be expensive to reduce pollution. For example, many kinds of waste could be used somehow, but the necessary reprocessing can cost a lot.

On the farms, many farmers keep their cattle in large pens rather than letting them roam the large fields. Land is so expensive that it is more economical to use the fields for crops. But in the open fields, the cattle's waste products are scattered and become natural fertilizer. In a confined area, too much of these waste products are dumped into too small an area. The soil cannot absorb all that waste, and some of it runs into the feed lots and can pollute bodies of water. With no natural fertilizer available in the fields, farmers must use chemical fertilizers, and much of that runs off the land and pollutes the water.

In industrial pollution, many factories burn coal, producing sulfur dioxide. Most of the sulfur in industrial smoke could be reused in the form of sulfuric acid. But the process is expensive and could cause the company to lose money to the extent that it might have to go out of business or would have to increase the price of its products.

The social causes of pollution are most often tied to our desire for convenience. There are countless synthetic products that pollute the environment that are used just to save time, money, or work.

For example, using throwaway packaging rather than easily recycled packaging, such as glass and metal containers, is not a good idea. This causes a buildup of trash that cannot be used again.

In addition, people find it more convenient to drive their own automobiles than to take public transportation. If more people were to take buses and trains, the public transportation systems would improve and the smaller number of polluting vehicles would cut down on air pollution drastically.

3
The Golden
1970s

President Nixon signed the final version of the National
Environmental Policy Act (NEPA) on January 1, 1970,
ushering in a new age of environmental protection. At that
time, not a single state had completed any plan for standards of pollution control. Then came the amendments to
the Clean Air Act of 1967, passed by Congress in 1970.

These amendments expanded the federal government's
role in setting and overseeing the standards for auto emissions. And they also established air-quality standards for
other pollutants. Now the government could really take
some action to control pollution from smokestacks. There
was now a timetable for cleaning up these emissions.

Nixon created another agency in 1970. He combined
most federal environmental, scientific, and data collections

into the National Oceanic and Atmospheric Administration (NOAA) to provide, as he said, "a unified approach to the problems of the oceans and the atmosphere." On October 3, this agency was established as a part of the Department of Commerce.

The Birth of the EPA

But perhaps the greatest pollution control occurrence of 1970 was the creation of the Environmental Protection Agency (EPA). The idea had gone through Congress in July of 1970, and Nixon created the agency by executive order on December 2. The EPA was to have the responsibility of maintaining the programs for clean air and water, pesticide control, and radiation monitoring. It combined the functions of fifteen federal agencies dealing with pollution and was created to streamline the government's conservation operations.

Water quality programs came from the Department of the Interior's Federal Water Quality Administration and HEW's Bureau of Water Hygiene. The programs of HEW's National Air Pollution Control Administration and the Bureau of Solid Waste Management were given to the EPA, making it the single most important federal agency dealing with pollution.

From both HEW and the Atomic Energy Commission came the programs to set environmental radiation protection standards, and the EPA also took on the responsibilities of the Federal Radiation Council. From the

The logo of the Environmental Protection Agency. It features a two-leafed flower, with abstract waves symbolizing water and a half-circle suggesting a rising sun.

Department of Agriculture came the authority to register and regulate pesticides. From the Food and Drug Administration came the authority to set limits on pesticide levels on and in food. From the Department of the Interior came its pesticide research program.

The EPA was also set up to police the standards of the Clean Air amendments of 1970. It was, in addition, directed to run a program to develop new ways of dealing with solid waste and to help state and local governments develop their own disposal systems under the Resource Recovery Act of 1970. Almost across the board, the EPA now had the authority to police pollution standards, and it had the power to fine polluters or shut them down. In addition, the EPA was to administer research grants to states, cities, and other government organizations and agencies. Nixon's new broom was ready to sweep clean.

Action Outside the EPA

The Occupational Safety and Health Administration (OSHA), a part of the Department of Labor, was established in 1971 during the presidency of Richard M. Nixon. It was set up as an outgrowth of the Williams-Steiger Occupational Safety and Health Act of 1970. Its purpose was to promote safe and healthful working conditions in all areas.

Part of its job was to deal with such pollutants as asbestos and lead in the workplace. OSHA has the power to fine employers who do not make required changes in their places of business or industry.

In 1971 the Food and Drug Administration began enforcing the Radiation Control for Health and Safety Act of 1968. This agency of the Department of Health and Human Services already had been administering the federal laws concerning the purity of food, the safeness of cosmetics, and the safety and efficiency of biological products and drugs, backing up the federal Food, Drug and Cosmetics Act of 1938 and the Drug Amendments Act of 1962. The FDA also promotes sanitary conditions in public eating places and ensures the safety of milk products and shellfish.

More Work for the EPA

The EPA continued to be assigned new jobs. Congress passed the Noise Control Act of 1972. It was the job of the EPA to set standards limiting noise from such things as construction equipment, motors, engines, and electronic devices. But the noise standards for aircraft became the job of the Federal Aviation Administration.

The Water Pollution Control amendments of 1972 extended federal control in all the waters of the nation. That meant the EPA could now establish limits on the amount of waste discharged into these waters. The task was to make rivers and lakes, according to Congress, "fishable and swimmable." It has not been completely successful, obviously, but the EPA helped things improve. Fish

A sailboat in clean water. The government has set a goal of making rivers and lakes clean for fishing and swimming, so that people can use and enjoy the waters.

returned to the Hudson River and also to the Detroit River, where ducks once died when they landed on its surface.

It was also in 1972 that the EPA rolled up its sleeves in a most important cause. The Environmental Pesticide Control Act of that year required that all pesticides be registered with the EPA. And one of the first outcomes of this action was that the EPA outlawed the pesticide DDT—a substance that was found to cause cancer in laboratory animals.

Things were going along quite well until 1974. That was the year of the Organization of Petroleum Exporting Countries (OPEC) oil embargo, and prices of gasoline zoomed upward, causing a runaway inflation. Business and industry, facing skyrocketing costs of obeying environmental requirements, begged Congress to ease up. And Congress did just that—postponing deadlines for conforming to EPA regulations.

But Congress did enact the Safe Drinking Water Act of 1974. This directed the EPA to set nationwide standards for drinking water quality, including safety limits on bacterial and chemical content.

In 1975 the EPA introduced the requirement that catalytic converters be put on automobiles to reduce their exhaust pollution. These converters can eliminate up to 90 percent of the harmful gases produced by cars.

Meanwhile, in 1975 the Nuclear Regulatory Commission (NRC) was organized during the administration of President Gerald R. Ford. Its function was to ensure that

The Safe Drinking Water Act was enacted to make sure that people can rely on our water's quality.

civilian use of nuclear energy was not dangerous to the health and safety of the American people. It was to oversee the construction of nuclear power plants and the use of radioactive materials in agriculture, medicine, and industry.

More Legislation

Two new pollution control laws were enacted by Congress in 1976.

The Toxic Substances Control Act gave the EPA the power to control the distribution and use of hazardous commercial and industrial chemicals. This bill was primarily aimed at PCB's (polychlorinated biphenyls)—a group of toxic chemicals commonly used in transformers, capacitators, and gas pipeline systems. The act also addressed itself to the controlling of poisonous wastes, including nuclear wastes.

The Resource Conservation and Recovery Act set the first regulations for the generation, transportation, and disposal of hazardous waste. This piece of legislation let the EPA oversee the handling of these materials. But it did not give the EPA the power to do anything about existing hazardous waste-disposal dumps.

Two more enactments came from Congress in 1977. The Clean Air Act amendments extended the deadlines for meeting several antipollution requirements. And the Clean Water Act permitted delays in getting rid of water pollution.

Things were not looking as good as they had. But at least the EPA was able to ban CFC's (chlorofluorocarbons) in aerosol sprays in 1979. Unfortunately, CFC's were still being used to make styrofoam, even though they were known to be at work breaking down the ozone layer.[1]

The outlook was bad at the end of the 1970s, but things were going to get worse.

4
The Gloomy 1980s

In 1980 Ronald Reagan was inaugurated as president, and it soon became apparent that he was not going to be an environmental champion. The first decade of the existence of the EPA had been an exciting decade. But things were going to change.

True, the Comprehensive Environmental Response, Compensation and Liability Act was passed by Congress in 1980. This act came as a reaction to many pollution disasters. Commonly known as the Superfund, it set aside $1.6 billion in a trust fund to pay for emergency and long-term cleanups of hazardous waste.

Bad News

But things were going to go downhill. From 1980 to 1983, EPA enforcement was relaxed, and the agency didn't effectively carry out its duties. This failure was caused in part by the high costs of cleaning up manufacturing plants. Some of them had to close down, and it looked as though the cleanup costs would drive the price of manufactured goods through the ceiling.

Early in 1981 Reagan set up a presidential task force, headed by Vice-President George Bush, to review all governmental regulations. That year the administration fired all of the professional staff of the Environmental Quality Council and cut the EQC's budget by more than 70 percent.

In May of 1981, Anne Gorsuch, a lawyer and a former Colorado state legislator, was appointed as administrator of the EPA. She had very little background in environmental matters, and one of her first acts was to replace twelve top-level assistant administrators, leaving only four assistant administrators in their jobs. The new group consisted of attorneys, lobbyists, and consultants for some of the very industries the EPA regulated. None had ever worked in environmental administration, and very few had any knowledge of government work. By November of 1982, one out of every five EPA employees had been fired, in what many environmentalists believed to be a policy of crippling the agency.

The Fall of the Administrator

The EPA administrator had recently been married, and it was as Anne Gorsuch Burford that she was cited by the House of Representatives for contempt of Congress in

On September 28, 1983, Anne Gorsuch Burford appeared before a House Energy and Commerce oversight subcommittee on Capital Hill. Burford, in her first appearance since resigning as head of the Environmental Protection Agency, said that President Reagan was poorly advised by the Justice Department in the administration's dispute with Congress over EPA documents.

December 1982. She had refused to submit certain documents requested by a House subcommittee, and she was suspected of mismanaging the Superfund program. She thus became the first subcabinet-level officer ever to be cited for contempt. As the investigation continued, more and more evidence surfaced of Burford's shifting of EPA funds to help Republican congressional candidates fund their campaigns. She had also prepared a "hit list" of EPA scientists unfriendly to the Reagan administration. In March 1983, on the instructions of President Reagan, she resigned.

William D. Ruckelshaus was appointed to be the new administrator. This was his second time on the job, since he had held the post when the EPA was formed. Just six months after he arrived, he had appointed new top officials and persuaded many scientists to come back to the agency. But he was not able to increase the EPA's budget. Actually, the funds were still being cut back by the Reagan administration. The administration also continued to veto his plans for new regulations, particularly on acid rain.

A Little Good News

A few positive things were still going on, however. In 1982 the federal Consumer Product Safety Commission had banned urea-formaldehyde foam, which had been used as insulation. As little as 0.1 ppm (parts per million) of formaldehyde in the air had been found to cause throat and lung irritation and other more serious conditions.

Many homes were found to have a 0.5 ppm concentration, and one high school in Oakland, California, was found to have 1.45 ppm.

Urea-formaldehyde foam had also been used in pressed-wood products, and fumes could escape from floors, furniture, and other pressed-wood items. It had been used in cosmetics, permanent-press clothing, upholstery, and carpeting, too.

More Bad News

A setback to the environment occurred in 1983 when a federal court overturned the 1982 Consumer Product Safety Commission's ban on urea-formaldehyde foam. The court ruled that only the EPA could ban carcinogenic (cancer-causing) materials.

The presidential task force, chartered in 1981, was dissolved in August of 1983. It had worked hard. Seventy-six regulations were either revised or eliminated, and many of these were EPA regulations. The Reagan administration also directed that any environmental regulation first had to calculate its benefits and compare the benefits with the cost of the regulation. Previously the EPA regulations were based only on the concern for the environment. By 1984, the EPA staff had been cut by 29 percent, and its funds had been cut by 44 percent, compared to the 1980 level.

Ruckelshaus, probably in frustration, resigned in January of 1985 and was replaced by Lee M. Thomas. At that time, it was estimated that as many as 50,000 lakes and streams in the United States and Canada were dead or dying because of acid rain pollution. And some scientists thought that as much as 30 percent of the forests of the Green Mountains in Vermont had died in the preceding 20 years because of acid rain.

Upturns

The EPA was back in action in 1986. It set the safety level for lead in drinking water at 50 ppb (parts per billion). The projected goal was that lead should drop to 20 ppb by mid-1988. The agency also identified a number of places in the country where lead contamination was a problem, pointing out that places with soft water tend to have higher lead levels.

Sick Buildings

Another new problem popped up in 1986. It was Sick Building Syndrome (SBS). The National Institute of Occupational Safety and Health (NIOSH) attributed 50 percent of employees' complaints about respiratory and sensory discomfort to inadequate ventilation and dirty air-handling systems. On the international level, the World Health Organization (WHO) estimated that 30 percent of the world's modern buildings were plagued by indoor air pollution.

Modern air-tight buildings present a problem: When sufficient outside air is not brought in and when

Modern buildings can harbor indoor air pollution if they are not monitored.

air-conditioning systems are not maintained properly, bad things happen. The result is recirculated stale air and miles of ducts contaminated by dust, fibers, fumes, cleaning chemicals and solvents, and mold.

The EPA estimated that some buildings had air two to five times more polluted than the outside air. Even the building that housed the EPA's headquarters qualified as a sick building. Eight EPA employees filed a $35 million lawsuit against the owner and manager of the building.

Meanwhile, the Safe Drinking Water Act of 1974 was amended in 1986. The new version included the requirement that the states develop ground water protection plans.

Asbestos

Another step forward came in 1986 when Congress passed the Asbestos Hazard Emergency Responses Act. This dictated that schools must control or remove asbestos following guidelines from the EPA. A fund of $100 million was allotted for the job in 1986, and another $47.5 million could be used in 1987.

In 1979 the government, through the EPA, had banned the use of asbestos as insulation. The 1986 law banned uses such as putting it under floor and roofing tiles and around heating pipes. But there were still asbestos products being made, such as in brake linings. The EPA wanted to ban them all, but there was a problem with

Canada. That country supplies most of the asbestos to the rest of the world.

Asbestos has been called the most widespread toxic substance in the United States. Not only was it used in insulation but also in patching compounds, textured paint, wrap for heating ducts and water pipes, floor and ceiling tiles, roofing shingles, cement, sand plaster, and brake linings.

Beginning in the 1950s, studies were pointing out that asbestos fibers can crumble, get into the air, and be inhaled, causing lung diseases. These fibers are like tiny glass splinters that can cause asbestosis, a condition that scars and stiffens the lungs. The disease also complicates breathing, and that can reduce the supply of oxygen to the lungs. The EPA estimated that in the early 1980s, from 8,000 to 10,000 deaths each year were caused by lung cancer brought on by asbestos exposure.

Also in 1986, Congress passed a $9 billion five-year toxic cleanup bill. This bill extended the Superfund, under which $1.6 billion had been spent in the previous five years. Hundreds of polluted sites across the country still had not been cleaned up.

The Reagan Vetoes

President Reagan gave the environment a little more trouble in 1986. In October, Congress approved an $18 billion renewal of the Clean Water Act. This provided funds for the construction of sewer systems and treatment

To reduce acid rain, the plan would reduce sulfur emissions from coal-fired power plants by 50 percent. Factories would be required to use cleaner fuel or install scrubbers (air pollution devices that use a spray of water or reactant, or a dry process to trap pollutants in emissions) to clean up the smoke. Alternative fuels for automobiles, such as methanol, ethanol, or natural gas, were to be encouraged. Auto manufacturers would be required to produce one million alternative-fueled cars by 1997.

Substantial reductions in tailpipe emissions and gasoline vapor levels were also proposed. Bush's plans would cost the automobile industry from $14 to $19 billion each year.

Expensive as that may have seemed, perhaps things were looking up.

5
How It Is Now

At the end of the EPA's second decade, people were beginning to think that George Bush was no Ronald Reagan. Perhaps we really did have an environmental president. Like an earlier wealthy eastern Republican, Theodore Roosevelt, he was an enthusiastic outdoorsman.

He also had more than a few conservationists on his team. C. Borden Gray, the White House counsel, was driving a methanol-fueled Chevrolet. Secretary of State James Baker was a supporter of a global-warming treaty. John Sununu, the White House chief of staff, was an expert on the greenhouse effect.

Most important of all, however, was the EPA's administrator, William Reilly. He began working at the Council on Environmental Quality in 1970 and so had been a conservationist for most of his adult life. Appointed to the EPA in 1989, he was an expert on wetlands, whaling,

The former administrator of the Environmental Protection Agency, William Reilly (left) being interviewed on the set of the EPA television

global warming, and toxic waste. Best of all, he had the president's ear. And he kept fighting for global treaties on our common pollution problems.[1]

Ozone Problems

Bad news about the ozone layer came in 1989. Since the 1970s the ozone layer over Antarctica had been thinning, and 1989 was the worst year yet. It had twice the thinning that had previously been observed by the National Aeronautics and Space Administration (NASA), letting in twice the amount of ultraviolet light. The ozone layer was also thinning over the Arctic, which meant a possible ozone hole there, too.

In October of 1990, some new warnings came from the National Aeronautics and Space Administration (NASA). A report from NASA's Goddard Space Flight Center stated that the ozone layer thinning above Antarctica was the worst in history. The previous month the reading was that chlorinated pollutants had destroyed up to 35 percent of the ozone layer above the Antarctic. This was three times greater than had been previously detected.

The ozone layer blocks the penetration of ultraviolet light to the earth's surface. With the depletion of the ozone layer, more radiation can reach the earth's surface. One of the chief results of excess ultraviolet radiation is skin cancer.

Melanoma is the most dangerous kind of skin cancer. In 1930, one American out of 1,500 developed melanoma. By 1986 the rate had gone up ten times—one out of every

150 people. By 2000 it is expected to hit one out of every 100 persons.

NASA gave us another warning in February 1992. Disaster might be coming with the development of a new ozone hole. But in May, the agency admitted that the hole never opened because of unseasonably warm temperatures in the Arctic.[2] And some scientists pointed out that air pollution might be of some benefit to the earth. Those same particles that cause acid rain perhaps help ward off global warming. Sulfate aerosols reflect sunshine, seed clouds, and create a cooler climate. This cooling just about equals the heating effect from the greenhouse gases such as carbon dioxide. And these same sulfates may be our best defense against the vanishing ozone layer.[3]

A New Clean Air Act

On November 15, 1990, President Bush signed his new Clean Air Act into law. The law lowered the allowable emission of sulfur dioxide to the level that was released in 1980. It also reduced permissible emissions of nitrogen oxides. This was a limitation on the cancer-producing air pollutants. Previously only benzene and six other chemicals were labeled as carcinogenic. The new law added 182 more suspicious chemicals.

Among the chemicals that under the law must be phased out of production were five CFC's, three halons (bromine-containing compounds), and carbon tetrachloride. This was to be done by the year 2000. The act also

The safe storage of hazardous waste is an important part of our war on pollution.

called for a slowdown in the production of HFC's (hydro-chlorofluorocarbons) by 2010 and total stoppage by 2030; HFC's had been considered to be replacements for CFC's as refrigerants.

There was more to the law. By 1995 the EPA had to produce a plan to reduce the cancer risk from air pollution in cities by 75 percent. The law also set up a Chemical Safety Hazard Investigation Board to check on chemical accidents, and work was to be done in a research program to evaluate the hazards in the accidental release of toxic chemicals.

Acid Rain

In March of 1986, the National Academy of Sciences reported that the burning of coal, gasoline, and other fossil fuels was definitely linked to the acid rain that had fallen in the northeast part of North America. Acid rain was responsible for killing fish, trees, and lakes in both the United States and Canada.

The new acid rain provision in the Clean Air Act signed by President Bush was based on a report, Project 88, formulated by Senator Tim Worth of Colorado and the late Senator John Heinz of Pennsylvania. Project 88 set a national goal for a 50 percent reduction in sulfur emissions. But this could be done with trade-offs.

Suppose an old plant burning high-sulfur coal finds it cannot reduce its own emissions to the desired level, even with expensive scrubbers. It could pay a utility company with newer equipment and low-sulfur coal to reduce its emissions by more than 50 percent, and the result would be the same sulfur reductions with a saving of $1 billion per year.[4]

Another Opinion

Nevertheless, an environmental bombshell exploded in 1990. The government's $535 million National Acid Precipitation Assessment Program (NAPAP) concluded its ten-year study of the acid rain problem. It was reported that we had been overstating the acid rain case for years. The report said that only 10.5 percent of the lakes in the Adirondack Mountains in New York state and only 6 to 7 percent of the streams in the Mid-Atlantic states owed their acidity to sulfur-containing compounds, which are common products in acid rain. And these were the areas considered the most harmed by acid rain.

The group also pointed out that acid rain had not reduced crop yields or harmed the majority of forests. Acid rain had caused the death of all fish in about 8 percent of the Adirondack lakes, but that was nowhere near the previous estimates. However, acid rain does cause haze, and 60 percent of the haze in the eastern United States and 30 percent of the haze in the West were caused by acid rain.

The report caused an uproar. Many organizations were not willing to believe it, even though many eminent scientists had been involved with it for ten years. The argument was so vehement that even CBS's *60 Minutes* devoted a segment to it.

Crackdowns

Early in 1991, there were some interesting judgments about environmental issues. After an investigation by the Federal Trade Commission (FTC), three firms agreed to modify their advertising. Zipatone, Inc., an art supply company, and Jerome Russell Cosmetics USA, Inc., manufacturers of hair spray, agreed to stop advertising that their spray cans contained "ecologically safe" or "ozone safe" propellants. The FTC had found that the cans contained a chemical that scientists believed was linked to the destruction of the ozone layer.

The FTC also caught up with a maker of disposable diapers. American Enviro Products, Inc., agreed that they would stop advertising their products as biodegradable (able to be broken down rapidly by living organisms under natural conditions and processes) after ten states had filed suits saying that the claim was false.

Legal Problems

In March of 1991 a most unusual development was reported. The EPA was trying to sue the Department of Energy for about $300,000. This amount would be in the form of a fine for failing to live up to a 1990 agreement with the EPA on what studies the department would carry out and what remedial actions it would take. In the agreement was a clause that a fine would be levied if the department was late on a deadline for action. And the Energy Department was late in cleaning up a thirty-seven-year-old uranium processing plant at Fernald, Ohio.[5]

The EPA found itself in legal trouble in 1991. In 1970, the Clean Air Act had said that the agency should identify and regulate "hazardous air pollutants." But the EPA had issued emissions standards for only seven chemicals in 20 years. A federal judge in San Francisco found the EPA in contempt for failing to set standards for radioactive air pollutants. Congress then ordered the agency to set standards for 189 chemicals.

Dr. Michael E. Porter of the Harvard Business School pointed out that the nations with the toughest environmental requirements often lead in the exports of related products. Germany has the tightest regulations concerning stationary antipollution control. And that country leads in the manufacturing and exporting of air pollution and other environmental technologies. About 70 percent of the air pollution control equipment sold in the United States is produced by foreign countries.

On the other hand, the United States leads in the areas where regulations are the strictest in this country, such as in pesticide control and the repairing of environmental damage. But more money is needed for environmental work all over the world.

At first, strict standards appear to raise costs and make companies less competitive. But these requirements call for companies to re-engineer their technologies. And this often reduces production costs while pollution is lessened.

For example, with the phaseout of PCBs, chemical companies in the United States are pioneers in finding substitutes. In conclusion, Porter said, "Turning environmental concern into competitive advantage demands that we establish regulations that stress pollution prevention rather than abatement or cleanup."

Less Ozone

Terrible news came in April 1991. The EPA's readings in the late fall, winter, and early spring indicated that over the previous ten years the ozone layer had become from 4.5 percent to 5 percent thinner. That was a figure twice as bad as had been predicted. It led to new predictions on skin cancer. The predictions of new cases of skin cancer over the next 50 years were that 12 million Americans would develop the condition. And 200,000 of them would die of the disease. This was in addition to the 8,000 deaths per year at that time. The previous 50-year prediction had been for about 500,000 new cancer cases of which 9300 would be fatal.[6]

Another ozone layer prediction came a few days later. The EPA expected concentrations of CFCs to continue to grow until the end of the century and reach a peak 12 to 30 percent above the present levels. This was mainly because of the fact that CFC's take years to rise from ground level to the ozone layer. But in about 2000, the levels should begin to subside. This is because we are controlling CFC's more effectively.

Dr. Clark Heath of the American Cancer Society commented, "There's no question that the ozone problem is really a problem that's not going to go away. One should take sun exposure seriously, particularly in the middle of the day." In the meantime, children in New Zealand were asked to eat lunch in the shade.[7]

In the face of all this, the National Academy of Sciences issued a report on April 10. Declaring that "despite the great uncertainties, greenhouse warming is a potential threat sufficient to justify action now," the academy called for several measures:

1. Adopt nationwide energy-efficient building codes.

2. Improve the efficiency of the U.S. automotive fleet through the use of an appropriate combination of regulation and tax incentives.

3. Strengthen federal and state support of mass transit.

4. Improve appliance efficiency standards.

5. Encourage public education and information programs for conservation and recycling.

6. Reform state public utility regulations to encourage electrical utilities to promote efficiency and conservation.

7. Sharply increase the emphasis on efficiency and conservation in the federal energy research and development budget.

8. Utilize federal and state purchases of goods and services to demonstrate best-practice technologies and energy conservation programs.[8]

The academy also analyzed the current climate changes and concluded that the following would happen:

1. If no effort is made to reduce emissions, greenhouse gas concentrations could continue to rise, doubling the preindustrial level by 2050.

2. This rise could ultimately increase average global temperature by 1° to 5° C (1.8° to 9° F).

3. Further increases in temperature are likely because the oceans release heat more slowly than land, and ultimately the temperature rise would be twice as high.[9]

Some Good News and Bad News

There were a few happier pieces of news in 1991. For one, the formaldehyde level in homes built since 1980 appeared to have dropped from 65 to 90 percent over the 1980 figure. Methane gas, a contributor to global warming, was building more slowly than it had been just nine years before.

Meanwhile, federal courts were facing a crisis in asbestos cases. Asbestos accounted for the largest number of civil cases in the courts, and there was a tremendous backlog. Plaintiffs were spending years in court without getting a penny. So on July 29, 1991, it was announced that something was going to be done about it. A panel of federal judges issued a ruling that consolidated some 26,639 actions in 87 federal districts.[10]

Disaster

Despite the federal government's concern for the planet, things can go wrong. One of the most complicated pollution disasters in which the federal government was involved began on March 24, 1989. The 987-foot (300-meter) tanker *Exxon Valdez* ran aground on Bligh Reef, 25 miles (40 kilometers) south of Valdez, Alaska. It spilled nearly 11 million gallons (40 million liters) of crude oil into Prince William Sound. The oil killed countless birds, fish, and other animals, and oil covered a huge area of the water. This was the largest tanker spill in the history of the United States.

The next day, the Exxon Shipping Company, the owner of the tanker, took full responsibility for the spill. One day later, on March 26, Alaska's Governor Steve Cowper declared a disaster emergency. Alaskan fishermen decided to ask for full compensation for the loss of their livelihood. Soon, 300 lawsuits were filed in state and federal courts against the Exxon Corporation. The people suing included not only fishermen but also seafood processors and distributors, Alaska natives, area businesses,

Exxon shareholders, environmental groups, towns and cities, and the state of Alaska. The suits involved a variety of maritime and environmental statutes.

On March 30, Exxon fired Joseph J. Hazelwood, the captain of the *Exxon Valdez,* after an investigation by the National Transportation Safety Board showed that his blood-alcohol content was above permissible levels for operating a commercial vessel.

By April 8, despite containment efforts, the spill had covered an estimated 3,100 square miles (8,029 square kilometers) and was leaking out of the sound to foul beaches along the Gulf of Alaska. On May 22, a grand jury indicted Hazelwood on three felony charges, holding him responsible for the damage.

On September 15, after spending one billion dollars, Exxon suspended its beach cleanup for the winter, claiming that it had left 1,100 miles (1,609 kilometers) of oiled beaches "environmentally stable." Alaskan officials disagreed and announced their own $21 million winter cleanup plan.

On February 27, 1990, a federal grand jury indicted Exxon and its shipping subsidiary on five criminal counts. If convicted on all counts, the company could be fined up to $1.6 billion and could be assessed an additional $600 million in penalties.

Hazelwood was found guilty on March 22 of a single charge of criminal mischief and other misdemeanor charges of operating a vessel while intoxicated and of reckless endangerment. In July of 1992, the charges against Captain Hazelwood were overturned by the Alaska Court of Appeals.

In mid-January 1991, Governor Hickel of Alaska proposed dropping all state and federal lawsuits against Exxon over damage done by the oil spill in exchange for $1.2 billion to restore and enhance Prince William Sound. On March 13, Exxon, Alaska, and the federal government announced the proposed settlement of the criminal and civil cases brought by the governments against the company.

But everything was not yet resolved. At the end of July 1991, more than 30,000 suits were still pending—claims filed by people and organizations other than the governments. Exxon was the defendant in about 200 of them. And if it lost all the cases, the company could lose over $100 billion. The other big loser could be the Trans-Alaskan Pipeline Liability Fund, which faced more than 20,000 claims and could have to pay damages of about $59 billion.[11]

In September 1991, after the Alaska legislature had rejected the proposed payments by Exxon, a federal district judge in Washington did the same.[12] On October 8, however, another federal district judge in Alaska accepted a $1 billion package of criminal and civil settlements from Exxon, but still, hundreds of lawsuits filed by private individuals, companies, and Alaskan villages were pending. However, the settlement also required Exxon to pay an additional $900 million over ten years to a trust fund to correct the damages.[13]

In April of 1992 it was discovered that the Valdez spill was far worse than had been originally recorded. Extensive damage to sea otters, killer whales, harbor seals, seabirds, and fish was reported. In addition, many archeological sites, including burial and home sites, had been damaged.[14]

Exxon had other problems. In 1990, while they were cleaning up some of the spill in Alaska, some other ugly things happened. An Exxon underwater pipe spilled 567,000 gallons (2,146,000 liters) into New York Harbor. This cost the company some $15 million dollars. Two days after that spill, Exxon spilled 24,000 gallons (90,840 liters) of heating oil through a hole in a barge docked in Bayonne, New Jersey, and then 3,500 gallons (13,247 liters) from a barge at its Bayway, New Jersey, refinery.[15]

The Fight Goes On

Apart from disasters, we can scarcely pick up a newspaper without reading about another environmental problem. Some of the headlines read:

- We May Be Losing The Ozone Layer
- The Earth May Be Warming
- There May Be An Increased Risk Of Skin Cancer
- Closing Military Installations Demands A Costly Cleanup

- Our Waters Are Still Not All "Fishable And Swimmable"

- Many Cities Do Not Have Adequate Secondary Sewage Treatment Plants

- Groundwater Contamination Continues

- Some Conditions, Such As Acid Rain, Hazardous Waste, And Global Warming May Be Getting Worse

But we are more aware of the problems than ever before. Government agencies are cracking down on polluters. Recycling is practiced in many places. Research continues. International cooperation is improving. Corporate America spends $115 billion a year to comply with federal environmental laws. If everybody helps, we will solve our problems.

6
The States Take Action

The Federal Government is not the only large organization that is concerned about the environment. Every state government has one or more watchdog agencies. These may be called the office of consumer protection, the department of health services, the department of public works, or something else entirely. State legislatures are also concerned with the elimination of pollution.

For many years, it has seemed as though the Pacific Coast states have been in the forefront of environmental legislation and action. California is the leader in air pollution wars—particularly with automobile emissions laws. Oregon and Washington were early proponents of solid waste and water pollution controls.

In the Northeast, there is an extraordinary amount of cooperation among the states. Many of them passed bottle

Traffic jams pour exhaust pollution into the air.

deposit laws at the same time. Several of them got together to formulate auto emissions standards as a group.

A Typical Northeast State

It would be impossible to give a complete rundown on the efforts of the states to protect the planet. But let's take a typical state to investigate. Connecticut is neither a leader nor a follower in environmental concerns. But, even so, much is going on there. Here are some of the concerns of the Constitution State, along with some suggested actions.

Forests. In areas that have been intensively built up, forests exist as only small, fragmented oases. This is a less-than-ideal situation for wild animals, many of whom range over large spaces. Certain local species of salamanders, for example, travel from forest to pond to breed in the spring. Water-dwelling turtles leave their homes once a year to lay their eggs in sandy areas. These treks become more and more hazardous as roads and highways continue to be built—separating the animals from their destinations.

The state urges citizens to do several things: Use organic fertilizers on lawns and gardens; avoid pesticides. Do not clear logs and foliage to make the woods look neater (underbrush and dead wood provide homes for salamanders and other creatures essential to the forest's food chain). Erect bird and bat houses.

Air. The state monitors the levels of six pollutants in the air over several communities. Ozone, sulfur dioxide, carbon monoxide, nitrogen dioxide, lead, and suspended particulates are all recorded. The biggest problem is ozone, which exceded the federal limit by 33 percent in the summer of 1991.

The state wants citizens to do two things. Organize car pools and walk or ride a bicycle whenever possible. And plant a tree.

Coastal Areas. Long Island Sound, off the coast of Connecticut, is home to sea turtles, seals, bluefish, lobsters, and clams. Protected from the strongest tides and bordered in places by fertile marshes and wetlands, it provides a breeding ground for wildlife and a resting place for more than 200 species of migrating birds.

The state suggests that its citizens refrain from two things—littering and pouring toxic chemicals like paint thinner and motor oil down the drain.

Fresh Water. There are several reservoirs and wells that provide water in the Constitution State. Pollutants that threaten the drinking water supply can come from leaky landfills, underground storage tanks (such as those at gas stations), road salt, agricultural chemicals, and faulty septic systems. Once they enter the soil, these contaminants make their way to the natural underground water supplies.

The state urges its citizens to do three things: Put a plastic jug and a few stones in toilet tanks to reduce the amount of water used per flush. Have motor oil and car batteries recycled at service stations and get rid of paint, bleach, and other chemicals at hazardous waste disposal

Solid waste spoils the beauty of autumn leaves beside a stream. We need to clean up our natural environment and stop littering.

facilities. Turn off the faucet while brushing teeth and install low-flow showerheads.

States and Problems

States also must cope with environmental disasters and other problems. Here are some of the highlights.

Love Canal. Beginning in the 1940s, the Hooker Chemicals and Plastics Corporation of Niagara Falls, New York, began to dump large quantities of poisonous chemicals. The site for the dump was an unfinished barge canal called Love Canal. This dumping went on for about twenty-five years until the canal was full, whereupon the company covered it with dirt.

That was a mistake, and later a bigger mistake was made when homes and a school were built on or near the covered-up canal. The trouble started in the 1970s when the Love Canal residents began to develop unusual health problems. Pregnant women were having unusually high numbers of miscarriages. Many babies were born with birth defects. High rates of cancer were discovered.

Scientists moved in to start testing. They took soil samples from the school playground and nearby homes and found more than eighty different chemical compounds there. And at least seven of them were carcinogenic (capable of causing cancer).

Love Canal was designated a disaster area by New York Governor Hugh L. Carey in August 1978. This enabled the state to make an offer to buy all the homes. By April of 1979, 235 of the 239 families who were affected had sold their homes and moved away. President Jimmy Carter then declared a state of emergency on May 21, 1980. By that time, another 710 families were believed to be in danger. These people were evacuated, many of them for good. The neighborhood had become a ghost town.

Times Beach. In the early 1970s, the tiny town of Times Beach, Missouri, began to use waste oil as a spray on dirt roads in order to keep down the dust. Unfortunately, the oil contained a chemical called dioxin. There are about seventy-five different compounds known as dioxin, which the federal government has called "one of the most perplexing and potentially dangerous chemicals ever to pollute the earth."

Dioxin can be found in some paints, varnishes, adhesives, and soaps. It also was found in the pesticide "Agent Orange" that affected so many people in Vietnam during the war there. Many war veterans are suing the manufacturer of Agent Orange, charging that the chemical ruined their health in various ways.

With regard to the symptoms caused by exposure to dioxin, Dr. Fred H. Shirley described some of them in the 1970s. "Many essentially acute symptoms have been observed in human beings. They include chloracne [a skin disease], digestive disorders, effects on some essential enzyme systems, aches and pains of muscles and joints, effects on the nervous system, and psychiatric effects."

Therefore, during 1982 and 1983, 2,400 people had to be evacuated from Times Beach, for a time, by the state of Missouri. This may have been a mistake. In August of 1991 the EPA admitted that there was evidence that dioxins were not the threat that they had seemed to be.

Three Mile Island. On March 28, 1979, a nuclear power plant almost caused another disaster. Located on Three Mile Island, near the city of Harrisburg, Pennsylvania, the plant had been operating only since 1978. Troubles in its construction and design had appeared almost immediately. The plant had to be shut down several times early in 1979 when the equipment failed. Then came the nearly disastrous day.

After yet another accident, a bubble of gas in one of the nuclear reactors was detected. Such a bubble could cause the worst accident imaginable. If it exploded, it could damage the cooling system. And without a cooling system operating, the temperature inside the reactor could reach 2,200° C (4,000° F). The reactor could then possibly melt down through the floor and into the earth below.

The result of that would be deadly radiation in the earth and in the air. Thousands of people would be in danger, and much of the state of Pennsylvania would become unlivable.

Governor Milton J. Shapp ordered that pregnant women and children under five years old were not to go within five miles of the plant. State officials began to draw up plans to move a million people out of the danger zone.

It was a blessing that these plans were not necessary. Engineers brought the reactor under control with only a small amount of radioactive gas being released into the air.

Colorado Fights Back. A strange series of happenings on the state front occurred in Colorado in 1989, and it illustrates how states can help in the pollution fight on a local level. The Adolph Coors Company, a Colorado brewing corporation, launched a "Pure Water 2000" campaign to give $500,000 in grants to groups and individuals to clean up lakes and streams.

But the Colorado Department of Health began to cite Coors for water pollution violations. At the end, the company had been cited 39 times, and in 1990, Coors agreed to pay $750,000 in fines for pumping contaminated waste water into Clear Creek, which runs past its brewery in Golden, Colorado.

Making Sense of Labels

Some of the industrial acceptance of environmental causes has led to a bit of confusion on the part of the consumer. We find "dolphin safe" stickers on tuna cans. We find "CFC-free" labels on spray cans. We find other statements: "environmentally friendly," "compostable," "photodegradable," and "biodegradable."

In May of 1991, a group of state attorneys general from eleven states criticized manufacturers for using confusing or downright misleading labels such as "environmentally friendly" or "safe for the environment." Other clearer terms such as "recyclable" or "ozone friendly" needed to be supported by reliable evidence. Hubert H. Humphrey III, the attorney general of Minnesota, said, "A new dynamic is at work—the ability of the consumer to choose not only just on the basis of price or color or size, or whatever, but also for ecological attributes."[1]

In December of 1991, the New Jersey Office of Consumer Protection began to send letters to dozens of companies asking them to prove the claims that they were making for their products. It was pointed out that "recycled" paper rarely means that it is paper made from products already used—it most often comes from industrial scraps. "Recyclable" often means nothing at all, because, with enough time and money, almost everything can be recycled. Other products with confusing labels were "nontoxic" moth balls, "reusable" lawn bags, "earth friendly" children's school kits, "environmentally safe" socks, and "nuclear-free" light bulbs.[2]

States and Automobile Pollution

Without any prodding from the federal government, top environmental officers from six New England states (Connecticut, Maine, Massachusetts, New Hampshire, Rhode Island, and Vermont), along with representatives from two other Eastern states (New York and New Jersey) and the District of Columbia, met in July 1991. They were to consider adopting new air pollution regulations for automobiles. They wanted to subject themselves to the strictest rules available—those written by the state of California.[3]

The state of California has long been the leader in pollution control, especially in the area of air pollution. Historically, other states with air pollution problems have copied California's regulations. This applies not only to auto emissions but also to emission controls of household adhesives, laundry starch, personal fragrance products, furniture polishes, paints, deodorants, and all-purpose cleaners.[4]

Among the things considered by the twelve states and the District of Columbia were emission testing during car acceleration, rather than when the car is idling, and requiring electronic catalytic converters—those devices on automobile engines that cut down on poisonous emissions.[5]

Unfortunately, by November the state of Connecticut had dropped out of this clean-air program. Governor Lowell P. Weicker, Jr., blamed the high cost of the enforcement of the new rules as the reason for not joining the other states.[6]

Finally the plan was adopted by nine states in the East (New York, New Jersey, Pennsylvania, Massachusetts, Virginia, Maryland, Delaware, New Hampshire, and Maine) and the District of Columbia.[7] And Governor Weicker announced that Connecticut would speed up its anti-air pollution plans on its own.[8]

7
On the International Front

In the 1970s and 1980s, the United States and many other countries from around the world became aware of the scope of the environmental problems facing the planet. During this period, many studies and findings indicated that most of the more serious problems were not just local or national but international problems. Many countries began to participate formally in meetings to discuss what to do about the pollution of the planet.

Recycling

One of the first meetings was held in Paris, France, in 1976. Representatives from thirty-five nations and international organizations attended a United Nations seminar on nonwaste

Rearranging solid wastes before recycling. The worker uses heavy
gloves and a face mask to protect himself.

technology. The subject was recycling. Not much was accomplished, but international concern had begun.

Acid Rain

The United States finally began to realize in the mid-1980s that acid rain was a serious international problem. In March of 1986, the National Academy of Sciences reported that the burning of coal, gasoline, and other fossil fuels was definitely linked to the acid rain that had fallen in the Northeast, killing fish and trees.

On March 18 and 19 of that year, President Ronald Reagan met with Canadian Prime Minister Brian Mulroney and reached an agreement between the United States and Canada on the acid rain problem. The two countries agreed to spend $5 billion to develop means of burning coal more cleanly.

Early Ozone Concerns

Representatives of twenty-four countries, including the United States, gathered in Montreal, Canada, during September of 1987 to discuss the continuing problem of the decreasing ozone layer in the atmosphere. The countries signed a treaty called the Montreal Protocol, which called for the freezing of the production of chlorofluorocarbons (CFC's); CFC's are the most important culprits in ozone depletion, and the agreement demanded a 50 percent reduction of world output of the chemicals that cause

CFC's by 1999. Production of another group of ozone-depleting compounds, halons, would be frozen by 1992.

On March 2, 1989, representatives of 123 nations, meeting in London, England, called for the speeding up of the freeze timetable for CFC's. Environmental ministers from twelve members of the European Community agreed in Brussels, Belgium, to ban all production of CFC's by the year 2000.

On May 2, 1989, representatives of eighty nations met in Helsinki, Finland, and supported a ban of all chemicals that endanger the ozone layer. The declaration called for CFC's to be phased out by the year 2000, at the latest. This was a tougher ruling than the Montreal Protocol of 1987, which merely called for CFC's to be cut in half by 1999.

On November 7, 1989, representatives of sixty-eight countries meeting in the Netherlands passed a resolution to stabilize levels of carbon dioxide emissions by the year 2000. This was the first ministerial-level conference ever held on the ozone problem. The theme of the meeting was discussion of the threat posed by the warming of the atmosphere, known as the greenhouse effect.

Global Warming

In 1988 came a bombshell announcement. The world was warming up. But this was not exactly a new idea. Dr. Roger Revelle of the Scripps Institution of Oceanography at La Jolla, California, had warned of global warming in the early

1950s. He had become concerned about the increase of atmospheric carbon dioxide from the global use of fossil fuels after testing air samples from atop a Hawaiian volcano.[1] The greenhouse effect is caused by atmospheric gases that prevent heat from the sun from radiating back from the earth, into space. Carbon dioxide is one of these gases.

Another warning came in 1990. In May of that year came a United Nations report prepared by scientists from thirty-nine countries. They issued a warning stating that global temperatures could rise by 1.1° C (2° F) within thirty-five years. They also forecast an increase of 3.3° C (6° F) by the end of the next century. To stabilize atmospheric concentrations at the present level, they said, carbon dioxide, methane, and CFC's would have to be reduced by 60 percent.

In June of 1990, yet another international group met in London, England. Representatives from fifty-nine nations agreed to stop producing CFC's and halons. Most of these countries were scheduled to stop production by the year 2000, according to the Montreal Protocol. But the developing countries of the earth had until 2010.

In February of 1992, scientists from 130 countries met in Washington, D.C., to discuss global warming. The big question that they needed to answer was whether the world was warming up drastically and was this warming part of a natural cycle or due to human activity?

What was surprising about the conference was that President Bush promised the scientists that the United

States would hold down the production of the gases that contribute to global warming. His goal was to cut back to about 2.3 billion tons (2.1 billion metric tons) per year by the year 2000. That was about the same amount as were produced in 1987. This was the first time that the United States federal government admitted that global warming was a problem.[2]

But later that year at a meeting in Nairobi, Kenya, negotiators from around the world met to consider global warming. The crucial issue was what to do about the rising emissions of carbon dioxide all over the earth. Although the United States emits more carbon dioxide than any other nation, the Bush administration favored waiting for further research on how dangerous the gas is.[3]

In early June, 1992, the most comprehensive international conference on the environment was held in Rio de Janeiro, Brazil. Attending were 118 heads of state and their aides, totaling some 35,000 participants. Two treaties were signed by 153 nations. The first was on global warming, and the second was on protecting the world's plant and animal species.

The first recommended curbing the emissions of carbon dioxide, methane, and other greenhouse gases. The second required inventories of plants and wildlife, and plans to protect endangered species.

The so-called "World Summit" proved one thing, regardless of how well the agreements are abided by. The environment has become prominent as a world issue.[4]

8
What You Can Do

As William K. Reilly, the former administrator of the Environmental Protection Agency, has said, "In the years ahead, our nation will face many troublesome environmental issues, domestic and international, and we will have to keep fine-tuning our approaches and re-adjusting our priorities to cope with them. But the basic principles of environmental stewardship do not and will not change. The time to act on them is now ... Think globally and act locally. You *can* make a difference."

That means that you and your classmates can make a difference.

1. You can familiarize yourself with the environmental stands of elected officials by attending campaign meetings and reading the newspapers when they outline their views on pollution. Your findings can be pointed out to voting members of your family or any other adult.

2. You can work for environmentally aware candidates on the national, state, or local level. All of them need the help that young people can give.

3. You can lobby officials through letter-writing. Help them understand the environmental problems that need attention.

4. You can survey your neighborhood and your town or city to see what needs to be done and find out where there are pollution problems.

All of these things can be done either on the individual or class level. Officials do pay attention.

Here are some suggested places to contact the people whose responsibility it is to clean up the planet.

You may also find local addresses and telephone numbers for federal agencies in the blue pages of your telephone book. Some of these agencies are the Food and Drug Administration, the Department of Health and Human Services, and your local United States senators and representatives.

Federal Government

Consumer Product Safety Division
5401 Westbard Ave.
Bethesda, Maryland 20207

Environmental Protection Agency
401 M St., SW
Washington, DC 20460

Federal Trade Commission
Pennsylvania Ave.
  at 6th St., NW
Washington, DC 20580

National Science Board
National Science Foundation
1800 G St., NW
Washington, DC 20550

National Aeronautics and
Space Administration
600 Independence Ave., SW
Washington, DC 20546

Occupational Safety and
Health Review Commission
1825 K St., NW
Washington, DC 20006

State Government

All states have agencies dedicated to the protection of the environment, such as the office of consumer protection, the department of health services, or the department of public works. State legislators are also concerned with the elimination of pollution. Addresses can be found in the blue pages of your telephone book.

Local Government

Many cities have pollution control agencies, too. Among them are the environmental protection boards, health departments, public works departments, and urban redevelopment commissions, although they may go by other names. Representatives to the city council

Removal of solid waste is carried out by city governments.

or board of representatives or other city legislators can also be contacted. Names and addresses can also be found in the blue pages of the telephone book.

Be sure to get out there and work for the future of the earth. Government agencies can only be as effective as the people they represent. Your opinion does count!

Epilogue

We are beginning to look at problems and to seek answers to our environmental and pollution problems. Governments, state by state, nation by nation, are beginning to realize the magnitude of the problems that face our planet. They are beginning to look at the problems and seek answers before we are overcome by disaster.

In the United States, since the 1950s the burning of coal has been dramatically cut back. Railroads, factories, and home furnaces, to a large extent, have switched from coal to cleaner oil and natural gas. Even in the case of those industries that still use coal, we often find that they are controlling the pollution from their furnaces.

Today, we seldom hear of diseases being caused by germs in city water supplies. This is because communities have built efficient water treatment plants.

We have become aware. We recycle and reuse. We actively try to clean up the environment. We test vehicles for air pollution and use lead-free gasoline. Even such corporations as Leggs Pantyhose and McDonald's have volunteered to cease using plastic and styrofoam for packaging their products.[1]

Things are looking up.

Glossary

abatement—Reduction in the degree or intensity of, or elimination of, pollution.

acid rain—A condition that occurs when sulfur and nitrogen compounds are changed to acids in the atmosphere and deposited on earth by rain, snow, or fog.

aerosol—A suspension of liquid or solid particles in a gas.

Agent Orange—A chemical plant killer used in the Vietnam War.

asbestos—A mineral fiber that can cause asbestosis or cancer.

asbestosis—A chronic disease associated with the inhalation of asbestos and affecting breathing.

biodegradable—Able to be decomposed by living organisms.

carcinogen—A substance that can cause cancer.

carcinogenic—Cancer-producing.

catalytic converter—An air pollution abatement device that removes pollutants from motor vehicle exhaust fumes.

conservation—Avoiding the waste of human and natural resources, and renewing them whenever possible.

dump—A site used to dispose of solid wastes without environmental controls.

ecology—The relationship of living things to one another and their environment; the study of these relationships.

emission—Pollution discharged into the atmosphere.

environment—The sum of all external conditions affecting the life, development, and survival of a living thing.

greenhouse effect—The warming of the earth's atmosphere caused by the buildup of certain gases.

herbicide—A pesticide designed to control or destroy plants.

insecticide—A pesticide designed to control the growth of, or kill insects.

inversion—An atmospheric condition caused by a layer of warm air preventing the rise of cooling air trapped beneath it.

ozone depletion—The destruction of the atmospheric ozone layer that shields the earth from ultraviolet radiation that is harmful to life.

pesticide—A substance or mixture of substances intended for preventing, destroying, or repelling any pest.

plastics—Non-metallic compounds that result from a chemical reaction and then are molded.

pollutant—Any substance introduced into the environment that negatively affects the usefulness of a resource.

pollution—The presence of matter or energy whose nature, location, or quantity produces undesired environmental effects.

radiation—Any type of energy formed in rays, waves, or energetic particles.

radioactive substances—Material that gives off radiation.

scrubber—An air pollution control device that uses a spray of water or reactant, or a dry process to trap pollutants in emissions.

toxic— Poisonous to living things.

Chapter Notes

Chapter 1

1. *The New York Times* (April 21, 1991), p. C3.

Chapter 2

1. Environmental Protection Agency, *Your Guide to the United States Environmental Protection Agency* (Washington, D.C., February 1989).

Chapter 3

1. Terri Shaw, *The New York Times* (June 11, 1991), pp. B1, B2.

Chapter 5

1. Harry Jaffe, "Point of Light," *Outside* (April 1990), pp. 41–46.

2. Bob Davis, "Hole in Ozone Didn't Develop, NASA Reports," *The Wall Street Journal* (May 1, 1992), p. B12.

3. Sharon Begley, "The Benefits of Dirty Air," *Newsweek* (February 3, 1992), p. 54.

4. Sharon Begley with Mary Hager, "Adam Smith Turns Green," *Newsweek* (June 10, 1991), p. 50.

5. Matthew L. Wald, "Energy Department Runs Afoul of Its Own Regulators," *The New York Times* (March 10, 1991), sec. 3, p. 3.

6. William K. Stevens, "Ozone Loss Over U.S. Is Found to Be Twice As Bad As Predicted," *The New York Times* (April 5, 1991), pp. A1, D18.

7. William K. Stevens, "Ozone Layer Thinner, But Forces Are in Place for Slow Improvement," *The New York Times* (April 9, 1991), p. C4.

8. William K. Stevens, "Urgent Steps Urged on Warming Threat," *The New York Times* (April 11, 1991), p. B12.

9. Ibid.

10. Stephen Labaton, "Judge's Panel, Seeing Court Crisis, Combines 26,000 Asbestos Cases," *The New York Times* (July 30, 1991), pp. A1, D4.

11. Mark Williams, "Valdez Spill Creates Jumble of Lawsuits," *The* (Stamford, Conn.) *Advocate* (July 28, 1991), p. B6.

12. Keith Schneider, "Exxon to Pay Higher Criminal Fines in New Pact to Settle Valdez Claims," *The New York Times* (October 1, 1991), p. A14.

13. "Judge Accepts Exxon Pact, Ending Suits on Valdez Spill," *The New York Times* (October 9, 1991), p. A14.

14. "Valdez Spill Toll Is Now Called Far Worse," *The New York Times* (April 18, 1992), p. 6.

15. Matthew L. Wald, "Exxon Adopts Preventive Measures in $10 Million Project to Avoid Spills," *The New York Times* (September 29, 1991), p. 30.

Chapter 6

1. Keith Schneider, "Can Shoppers Tell If Something Is Really Good for the Planet?" *The New York Times* (July 14, 1991), sec. 4, p. 4.

2. Michael Specter, "Making Sense of Labeling on Products," *The New York Times* (December 16, 1991), pp. B1, B7.

3. Matthew L. Wald, "When the EPA Isn't Mean Enough About Cleaner Air," *The New York Times* (July 21, 1991), sec. 4, p. 5.

4. Matthew L. Wald, "California Air Agency Limits Personal Goods," *The New York Times* (January 10, 1992), p. A12.

5. Susan Eaton, "Region Considers Tough Auto Pollution Rules," *The* (Stamford, Conn.) *Advocate* (July 16, 1991), pp. 1, 8.

6. Matthew L. Wald, "Weicker Drops Out of Regional Clean-Air Program," *The New York Times* (November 8, 1991), p. B5.

7. Matthew L. Wald, "9 States in East Plan to Restrict Pollution by Cars," *The New York Times* (October 30, 1991), pp. A1, A23.

8. Daniel P. Jones and Michele Jacklin, "Weicker Speeds Up Decision on New Anti-Smog Standards," *The* (Stamford, Conn.) *Advocate* (November 25, 1991), p. 5.

Chapter 7

1. Walter Sullivan, "Roger Revelle, Early Theorist in Global Warming and Geology," *The New York Times* (July 17, 1991), p. B5.

2. Keith Schneider, "U.S. Accepts Greenhouse Target," *The New York Times* (February 5, 1991), p. C9.

3. William K. Stevens, "At Meeting on Global Warming, U.S. Stands Alone," *The New York Times* (September 10, 1991), pp. C1, C8.

4. James Brook, "U.N. Chief Closes Summit With an Appeal for Action," *The New York Times* (June 15, 1992), p. A8.

Epilogue

1. Eric N. Berg, "McDonald's Planning to Cut Its Garbage," *The New York Times* (April 16, 1991), p. B2.

Bibliography

Botkin, Daniel B. *Discordant Harmonies.* New York: Oxford University Press, 1990.

Brown, Lester R., Christopher Flavin, and Sandra Postel. *Saving the Planet.* New York: Norton, 1991.

Center for Investigative Reporting and Bill Moyers. *Global Dumping Ground.* Washington, D.C.: Seven Locks Press, 1990.

Dorf, Richard C. *Energy, Resources and Policy.* Reading, Mass.: Addison-Wesley, 1978.

Ehrlich, Paul R. and Anne H. *Healing the Planet.* Reading, Mass.: Addison-Wesley, 1978.

Environmental Protection Agency. *Meeting the Environmental Challenge.* Washington, D.C.: EPA, 1990.

———. *Your Guide to the United States Environmental Protection Agency.* Washington, D.C.: EPA, 1989.

Environmental Protection Agency/Consumer Product Safety Commission. *The Inside Story; A Guide to Indoor Air Quality.* Washington, D.C.: EPA/CPSC, 1988.

Gay, Kathlyn. *Silent Killers.* EPA/CPSC, 1988.

Lambert, Mark. *The Future for the Environment*. New York: Bookwright Press, 1986.

Law, Kevin J. *The Environmental Protection Agency*. New York: Chelsea House, 1988.

MacEachern, Diane. *Save Our Planet: 750 Everyday Ways You Can Help Clean Up the Earth*. New York: Dell, 1990.

Markham, Adam. *The Environment*. Vero Beach, Fla.: Rourke, 1988.

Nance, John J. *What Goes Up*. New York: Morrow, 1991.

Norsgaard, E. Jaediker. *Nature's Great Balancing Act: In Our Own Backyard*. Freeport, Maine: Cobblehill, 1990.

Paehlke, Robert C. *Environmentalism and the Future of Progressive Politics*. New Haven, Conn.: Yale University Press, 1989.

Peckham, Alexander. *Resources Control*. New York: Glouster Press, 1990.

Porritt, Jonathon. *Save the Earth*. Atlanta, Ga.: Turner, 1991.

Pringle, Lawrence. *Global Warming*. New York: Arcada, 1990.

Purcell, Arthur H. *The Waste Watchers*. Garden City, N.Y.: Anchor Press/Doubleday, 1980.

Schweitzer, Glenn E. *Borrowed Earth, Borrowed Time: Healing America's Chemical Wounds*. New York: Plenum, 1991.

Woods, Geraldine and Harold. *Pollution*. New York: Franklin Watts, 1985.

Index

BOSTON PUBLIC LIBRARY

3 9999 02090 496 5

WITHDRAWN
No longer the property of the
Boston Public Library.
Sale of this material benefits the Library.

① 12/99

Boston Public Library

WEST ROX
BRANCH LI

WR BR

HC110
.E5
A95
1993

The Date Due Card in the pocket indicates the date on or before which this
book should be returned to the Library.

Please do not remove cards from this
pocket.